Let's Vote!

Learning to Use Simple Bar Graphs

Roland Graham

Rosen Classroom Books & Materials
New York

Voting is a way to find out what most people in a group want.

Each person in a group gets one **vote**.
Then the votes are counted to see what
most people want.

A class can vote to pick the class **president**. Four people in this class want to be president.

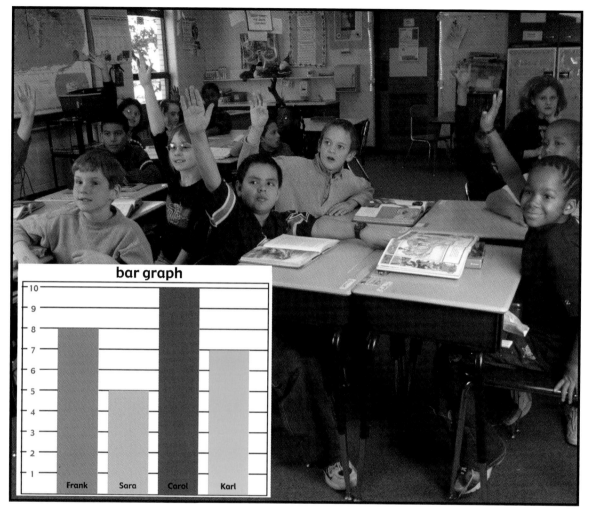

There are 30 people in the class. After the class votes, you can use a **bar graph** to show how many votes each person got.

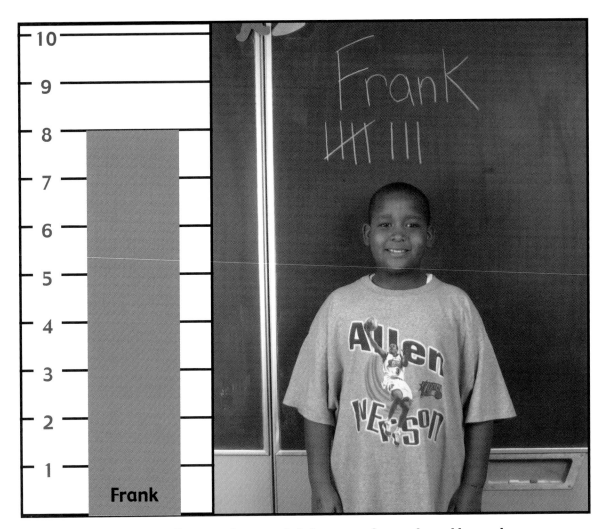

Frank gets 8 votes. We color in the bar
next to Frank's name up to the number 8.

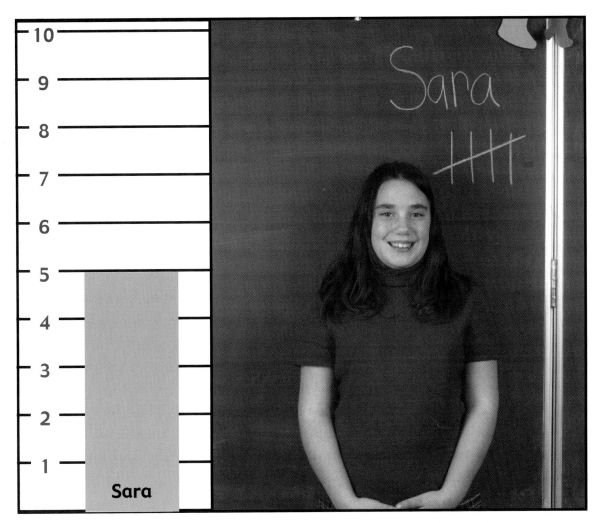

Sara gets 5 votes. We color in the bar next to Sara's name up to the number 5.

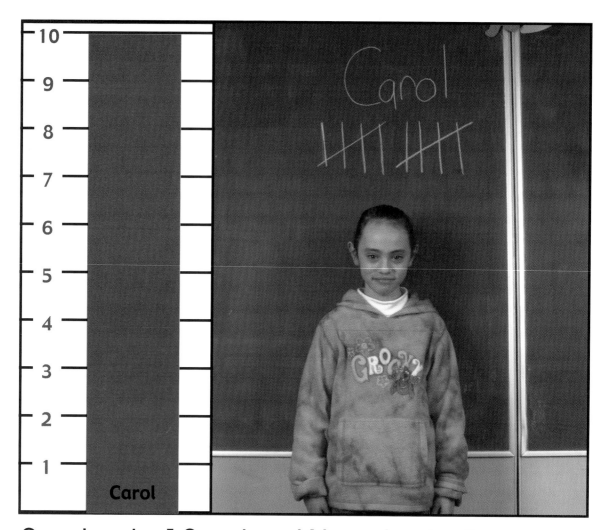

Carol gets 10 votes. We color in the bar next to Carol's name up to the number 10.

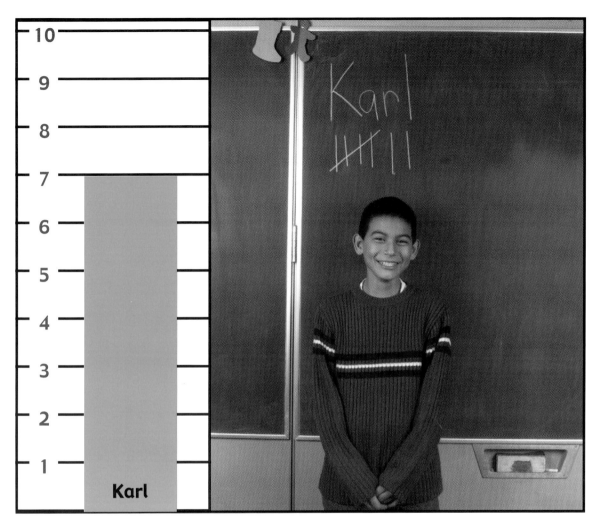

Karl gets 7 votes. We color in the bar next to Karl's name up to the number 7.

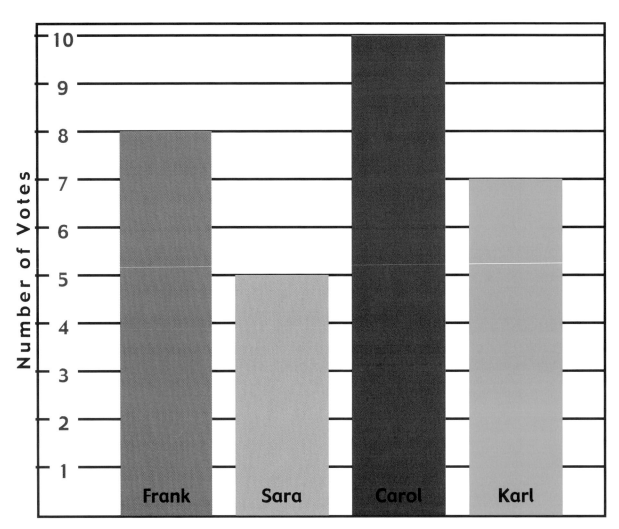

This bar graph makes it easy to see who got the most votes.

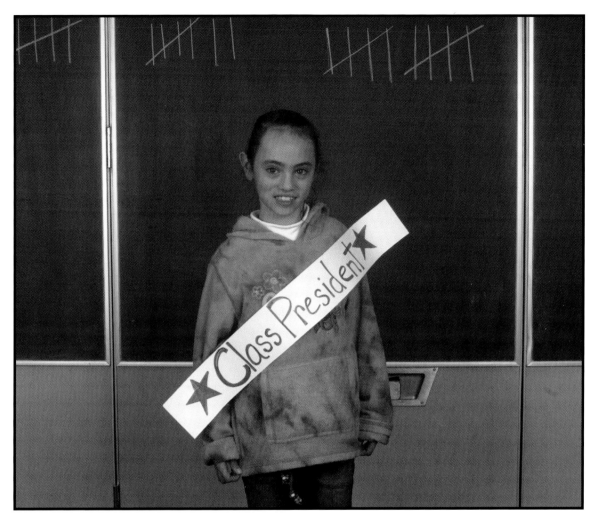

Carol got the most votes, so she is the new class president!

Glossary

bar graph (BAHR GRAF) A chart that uses bars to show how many of something.

president (PREH-zih-duhnt) The leader of a group, class, or country.

vote (VOHT) A person's pick for a leader, thing, or action.

voting (VOH-ting) Letting everyone in a group have a say in who will be the leader or what the group will do.